GETTING TO KNOW THE WORLD'S GREATEST ARTISTS

EL GRECO

WRITTEN AND ILLUSTRATED BY MIKE VENEZIA

CHILDREN'S PRESS®
A DIVISION OF GROLIER PUBLISHING
NEW YORK   LONDON   HONG KONG   SYDNEY
DANBURY, CONNECTICUT

To Victor Haboush, my good friend–
Thanks for your inspiration.

Cover: *Burial of Count Orgaz*, by El Greco (Doménikos Theotokópoulos). 1586. Santo Tome, Toledo, Spain. © Giraudon/Art Resource.

Project Editor: Shari Joffe
Design: Steve Marton

Library of Congress Cataloging–in–Publication Data

Venezia, Mike.
    El Greco / written and illustrated by Mike Venezia.
        p. cm. — (Getting to know the world's greatest artists)
    Includes bibliographical references and index.
    Summary: Examines the life and work of Doménikos Theotokópoulos, the sixteenth-century artist who created his greatest works in Spain, where he was known as "El Greco."
    ISBN 0-516-20586-2 (lib. bdg.)   0-516-26243-2 (pbk.)
    1. Greco, 1541?–1614 —Juvenile literature. 2. Painters — Spain —
–Biography—Juvenile literature. [1. Greco, 1541?–1614.
2. Artists.] I. Title. II. Series: Venezia, Mike. Getting to know the world's greatest artists.
ND813.T4V45   1997
759.6—dc21
[B]
                                 96-40223
                                    CIP
                                      AC

Portrait of a Man, by El Greco (Doménikos Theotokópoulos). Oil on canvas. 52.7 x 46.7 cm. Purchase, Joseph Pulitzer Bequest, 1924.
© The Metropolitan Museum of Art.

Doménikos Theotokópoulos was born on the Greek island of Crete in 1541. As a young man, he traveled to Italy to study the master artists there. Doménikos then traveled to Spain, where he created his greatest works of art. In Spain, Doménikos was nicknamed El Greco, which is Spanish for "the Greek."

Many of El Greco's paintings are based on religious stories from the Bible, especially stories about the life of Jesus Christ. People all over Europe wanted these types of paintings for their churches and homes.

Despoiling of Christ,
by El Greco (Doménikos
Theotokópoulos). 289 x
147 cm. Alte Pinakothek,
Munich, Germany.
© Scala/Art Resource.

El Greco's artwork was so different and original, it puzzled and amazed the people of his time. It still amazes people today! El Greco was able to create a feeling of wonder or fear or excitement or love in his paintings.

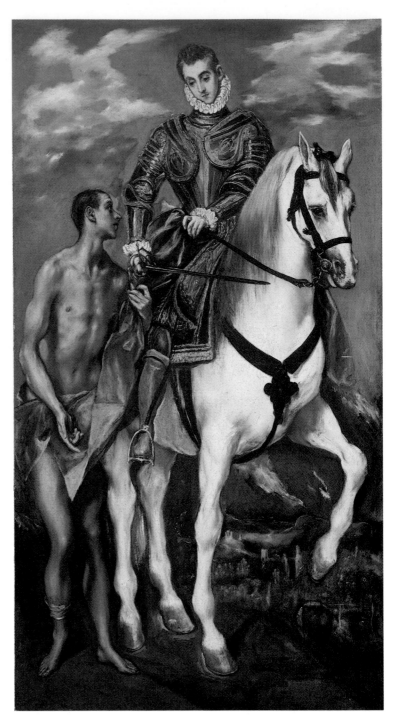

Saint Martin and the Beggar, by El Greco (Doménikos Theotokópoulos). 1597-99. Oil on canvas, wooden strip added at bottom. 76 1/8 x 40 1/2 in. © 1996 Board of Trustees, National Gallery of Art, Washington D.C., Widener Collection.

He did this by sometimes twisting and stretching out his figures to create movement. He used crackling, electric colors and mysterious lighting that seemed as if it came from another world— or from a science-fiction movie.

Adoration of the Shepherds, by El Greco (Doménikos Theotokópoulos). 1612–1614. Oil on canvas. 320 x 180 cm. Museo del Prado, Madrid, Spain. © Scala/Art Resource.

Not much is known about El Greco when he was growing up. He most likely learned to draw and paint at one of the many monasteries in Crete. A monastery is a place where people called monks live and study religion very seriously. During El Greco's time, monks also taught children reading, math, religion, and art.

El Greco probably started out learning to
paint icons. Icons were little religious paintings.
It seemed like everyone in Crete wanted an
icon to carry around or pray to in their home.
Artists in Crete were kept busy all the time.

Christ Redeemer, by John Metropolitos. 1393-94. Gallery of Art, Skopje, Macedonia. © Giraudon/Art Resource.

Icons were done in the ancient Byzantine style of art. The people shown in these paintings usually looked flat and stiff. But their mysterious eyes, as well as the rich colors used, gave icons a strange beauty and power.

When El Greco was a young man, he decided to leave Crete and travel to the Italian city of Venice. El Greco wanted to learn to draw the human figure in a more natural, realistic way. He also wanted to find out how the Italian artists gave a three-dimensional feel to their paintings. These artists created background spaces that seemed to go way into the distance. This was much different from the flat, Byzantine art that El Greco knew from home.

Venice was an exciting seaport city in the 1500s. Ships from all over the world came there to buy and sell things. There were celebrations and boat parades all the time. El Greco was fascinated by the large oil paintings that filled the churches and palaces there.

Venice: The Doge's Palace and the Molo from the Basin of San Marco, by Francesco Guardi. c. 1770. Oil on canvas. 58.1 x 76.4 cm. © Reproduced by courtesy of the Trustees, The National Gallery, London.

The Wedding at Cana, by Paolo Veronese. 1562-63. Canvas. 666 x 990 cm. From the Benedictine Convent of San Giorgio Maggiore, Venice, Italy. Louvre, Paris, France. © Erich Lessing/Art Resource.

Oil paint was new to El Greco. He had worked only with water colors before. The Venetian artists loved oil paints because they came in brighter, richer colors. Also, oil paints could be either brushed on in thick globs, or thinned out so that the colors would swirl together and create an exciting look.

Assumption of the Virgin, by Titian (Tiziano Vecelli). 1516–18. Oil on panel.
690 x 360 cm. Santa Maria Gloriosa dei Frari, Venice, Italy. © Scala/Art Resource.

El Greco was influenced by Venetian artists like Titian and Tintoretto. He learned about beautiful new color combinations from Titian, and he saw how Tintoretto filled his paintings with action.

In the Tintoretto painting shown below, people seem to be doing things all over the place. Your eyes go from the front to the back and up and down to different scenes. Tintoretto also used an eery, supernatural light that came from people's halos and beams from heaven.

Last Supper, by Jacopo Tintoretto. Oil on canvas. 365 x 568 cm.
San Giorgio Maggiore, Venice, Italy. © Cameraphoto/Art Resource.

When El Greco felt he had learned all he could in Venice, he traveled to Rome, another important Italian art center. In Rome, El Greco studied Renaissance masters like Raphael and Michelangelo.

El Greco also met lots of important people there. Some of them were from Spain. El Greco's Spanish friends told him about a huge palace being built by the king of Spain, Philip II. The king wanted all kinds of paintings and artwork for his new palace.

El Greco thought it might be a good idea to go to Spain and try to get some work there. He also thought it might be a good idea to leave Rome, because he had made a lot of people angry when he offered to redo one of Michelangelo's most famous paintings, *The Last Judgment*.

El Greco respected Michelangelo's powerful sculptures, which were filled with life, but he wasn't that crazy about some of Michelangelo's paintings.

When El Greco first arrived in Spain, he stopped in the city of Toledo. El Greco fell in love with Toledo. There was something mysterious and exciting about its ancient buildings and rugged countryside. El Greco showed the way he felt about Toledo in *View of Toledo*, one of the most fantastic landscape paintings ever done.

Light from the stormy, swirling sky seems to make Toledo glow like the surface of the moon. El Greco often included scenes of his favorite city in the backgrounds of other paintings.

View of Toledo, by El Greco (Doménikos Theotokópoulos). c. 1600. Oil on canvas. 121.3 x 108.6 cm.
© The Metropolitan Museum of Art, H.O. Havemeyer Collection, Bequest of Mrs. H.O. Havemeyer, 1929.

Things went pretty well for El Greco when he got to Toledo. Right away, he was asked to make a large painting. It's interesting to compare El Greco's *Assumption of the Virgin,* on the next page, with Titian's painting of the same subject, which appears on page 14 of this book. Even though El Greco was influenced by Titian, in his painting he started to do different things that made him a great and original artist.

El Greco began to get rid of the spacious backgrounds the Italian artists had used. He made his figures more stretched out, and used unusual and beautiful color combinations.

The Assumption of the Virgin,
by El Greco (Doménikos
Theotokópoulos). 1577.
Oil on canvas. 401.4 x 228.7 cm.
© 1996, The Art Institute
of Chicago, Gift of Nancy
Atwood Sprague in memory
of Albert Arnold Sprague.

El Escorial, the royal palace built by King Philip II, 1563-84. Photograph by Gian Berto Vanni. Escorial, Madrid, Spain. © Vanni / Art Resource.

El Greco's first paintings in Toledo were well liked. The king of Spain heard about El Greco's work, and asked him to do a painting for his new palace in the nearby city of Madrid.

El Greco was thrilled. Only the best artists in the world were asked to paint pictures for the king. El Greco started right away on a painting called *The Martyrdom of Saint Maurice*. Unfortunately, when King Philip saw the painting, he didn't like it very much.

The Martyrdom of St. Maurice, by El Greco (Doménikos Theotokópoulos). 1580–82. Oil on canvas. 448 x 301 cm. Escorial, Madrid, Spain. © Scala/Art Resource.

Maybe the king didn't understand El Greco's unusual lighting and colors or the way he stretched his figures out. The king may have felt this painting was too crowded and had too much going on in it. Whatever the reason, King Philip had the painting taken down and redone by another artist. He never asked El Greco to do another painting again.

El Greco was very upset, but luckily, people in Toledo still loved his work. He was asked to do lots of new paintings. El Greco started doing wonderful portraits. Not only was he able to show what people really looked like, but his paintings also give you a feeling of what these people might be like in real life.

Portrait of a Nobleman with his Hand on his Chest, by El Greco (Doménikos Theotokópoulos). c. 1580. Oil on canvas. 81 x 66 cm. Benaki Museum, Athens, Greece. © Scala/Art Resource.

Antonio de Covarrubias y Leive, theologian, canon of the Cathedral of Toledo, by El Greco (Doménikos Theotokópoulos). Oil on canvas. 126 x 86 cm. Louvre, Paris, France.© Erich Lessing/Art Resource.

Portrait of a Lady, by El Greco (Doménikos Theotokópoulos). Oil on wood.
© Philadelphia Museum of Art, The John G. Johnson Collection.

The painting above, of Jerónima de Las Cuevas, shows that she was a quiet, sweet lady who was very pretty and maybe a little bit sad at times.

El Greco and Jerónima fell in love and had
a son they named Jorge. El Greco included
his son in many paintings from the time Jorge
was a baby until he grew up.

In one of El Greco's paintings, Jorge is shown holding a torch and pointing to the scene behind him. The scene Jorge is pointing to is the *Burial of Count Orgaz.*

In this painting, the generous and kind count is shown being buried in his suit of armor. The painting is one of El Greco's greatest masterpieces. El Greco didn't put a background in the painting, which kind of pushes the people out toward you. It almost gives you the feeling that the people are right there in front of you. He crowded the bottom half of the painting with figures, but opened up the space above, so that angels and clouds and the count's soul are swept up to heaven.

Burial of Count Orgaz could have been a sad scene, but the way El Greco painted it lets you know that the count will be welcomed and well taken care of when he gets to heaven.

As the years went on, El Greco's people and scenes became filled more and more with crackling light and color. El Greco painted with more emotion and swirling movement.

St. Joseph and the Christ Child, by El Greco (Doménikos Theotokópoulos). 1597-99.
Oil on canvas. 289 x 147 cm. Museo de S. Cruz, Toledo, Spain. © Bridgeman/Art Resource.

The way he painted hands reminds some people of flickering flames or birds' wings. In some paintings, El Greco's little angels look almost like soap bubbles gurgling out of the clouds.

Madonna and Child with Saint Martina and Saint Agnes, by El Greco (Doménikos Theotokópoulos). 1597-99. Oil on canvas, wooden strip added at bottom. 6 1/8 x 40 1/2 in. © 1996 Board of Trustees, National Gallery of Art, Washington, D.C., Widener Collection.

The Feast in the House of Simon, by El Greco (Doménikos Theotokópoulos). c.1610-14. Oil on canvas. 143.3 x 100.4 cm. © 1996, The Art Institute of Chicago, Joseph Winterbotham Collection.

El Greco died in his favorite city, Toledo, at the age of 74. He combined the things he had learned from Byzantine and Italian artists, and then he added his own special touches to create some of the world's most beautiful art.

The works of art in this book came from:

Alte Pinakothek, Munich, Germany

The Art Institute of Chicago, Chicago, Illinois

Benaki Museum, Athens, Greece

Escorial, Madrid, Spain

Gallery of Art Skopje, Macedonia, Greece

Louvre, Paris, France

Medici Chapel, San Lorenzo, Florence, Italy

The Metropolitan Museum of Art,
New York, New York

Museo de S. Cruz, Toledo, Spain

Museo del Prado, Madrid, Spain

The National Gallery, London, England

National Gallery of Art, Washington, D.C

Philadelphia Museum of Art, Philadelphi
Pennsylvania

Santa Maria Gloriosa dei Frari, Venice, Ita

Santo Tome, Toledo, Spain

San Giorgio Maggiore, Venice, Italy